Grow Through It,
and
Glow From It!

Grow Through It, *and* Glow From It!

TAKESHA BROWN

Copyright © 2022 by Takesha Brown.

ISBN: 978-1-7379009-7-9

All rights reserved. No part of this book may be reproduced or transmitted in any form or by any means, electronic or mechanical, including photocopying, recording, or by any information storage and retrieval system, without permission in writing from the copyright owner.

Contents

Foreword 7
Introduction 9

Chapter 1 – When God Spoke To Me 11
Chapter 2 – The Trials of Life 23
Chapter 3 – Ask, Seek, Knock 31
Chapter 4 – Spiritual Gifts 37
Chapter 5 – Disciplining Yourself 43

Prayer of Salvation 55
About the Author 57
Acknowledgments 59

Foreword

Takesha Brown's Foreword
by Dr. Kishma George

Mere words cannot describe how delighted and overjoyed I am about this book. Takesha is a beautiful soul and has endured so much. Everyone has a testimony, but when you have lived in a constant storm and you still manage to smile, get up and to keep fighting; you learn to grow. The power behind this is from our Amazing God. God will equip you for battle and sustain you. Takesha has persevered and shares in her new book, Grow Through It, Glow From It; how to push through the pain. Her heart for God and her love for people, allows her to speak directly to the heart of each of you. This book is filled with personal experiences, trials, and expressions of some of the most fearful moments in her life. She believes that there are things that happen in our lives that we must learn in order to keep pushing and "grow." After we grow, we can "glow."

Grow Through It, Glow from It, will inspire, encourage, and motivate you to keep on going. Giving up is not an option, as long as you keep your heart and mind on the Lord; seeking Him for guidance and assistance: being reminded to GROW, then GLOW!

Dr. Kishma George

Introduction

As I dig deep into my past and reflect on the many obstacles I've faced, I see the evidence of God's hand on my life. His fingerprints were upon me as a teen mom, with various illnesses, panic attacks and throughout my life. Much to my surprise and like many stuck in the house during the pandemic, I used the idol time indoors to reflect on my life. I decided to embark on life, take what God handed me and move forward. So, after a 24-year hiatus, I decided to pursue my purpose and enroll in school. This might sound crazy to you, but I did it.

Once I was accepted into the institution of my choice, I identified my passion and learned that I thoroughly enjoyed writing. Becoming an author is something I always wanted to do. I encourage you to allow your fingers to turn the pages of life with me as I share with you how to get up after you've been knocked down by the trials of life. *Grow Through It, Glow From It,* is my testimonial introduction to the world. No matter what I faced, I allowed God to be my strength, healer and provider and came out of it shining! You can do the same! Glow sister glow! Glow brother glow! This is not the time to quit, this is not the point in life where you stop. This is the time to keep going; there is sunshine on the other side of darkness. Together we will Grow and Glow!

Chapter 1

When God Spoke To Me

*"At 15, I got my first job and by 17,
I was pregnant."*

When I was in my early twenties, I remember being at a women's conference at my church. Each room was set up with different workshops, organized by topics. This was the first time I had ever been to an event like this. I attended several workshops that resonated with me.

After listening to each speaker, I remembered feeling so inspired that I visioned one day being able to imbue others. It was at that moment, God spoke to me, saying, "You will do this one day." I was in awe and welcomed the presence of God. I could not wait for the opportunity to pour into others. I couldn't believe that God would choose me to help and encourage other women, just as these women were doing for me. Tears rolled down my eyes and God's spirit filled the room, suddenly I felt bold, courageous, and ready to conquer anything God sent my way.

Not long after God spoke those words to me, I forgot about what He promised me and I fell back into my usual pattern of life. Distractions came and as we all know, you can hear a good word, but when you hesitate to act on it, without notice; you forget everything God told you. And that's exactly what I did. Jesus explained this in Matthew 13:19-22 NIV, *When anyone hears the message about the kingdom and does not understand it, the evil one comes and snatches away what was sown in their heart. This is the seed sown along the path. The seed falling on rocky ground refers to someone who hears the word and at once receives it with joy. But since they have no roots, they last only a short time.*

When trouble or persecution comes because of the word, they quickly fall away. 22 The seed falling among the thorns refers to someone who hears the word, but the worries of this life and the deceitfulness of wealth choke the word, making it unfruitful.

Years later, I began to listen to Juanita Bynum on her Facebook Live, it was called @3WithMe. I learned so much from the program, it was such a blessing. I needed the teaching that the Woman of God gave more than ever. I needed direction. For years I seemed to be lost or stagnant. I was trying to get on track, and I knew God was leading me in another direction.

I was listening to Dr. Bynum teach about the numerological meaning of number 52. She stated that Nehemiah was instructed to build the wall in 52 days, and how 52 is the number of Introspection, the ability to hear what the Lord is saying. It is the number to fight. The devil gets mad when you decide to follow God. I decided to sow a $52 seed that night. God began to speak words of encouragement to me. He said, "Finish the work, finish the assignment!" He said, you may not always feel me, but I am here; I will never leave nor forsake you; don't give up; this is not the time to become a quitter. This is the time to be a finisher!

Backstory. Nothing was handed to me on a silver platter. With many obstacles in front of me, I continued to pray, attend church, worship, and read the Word. I loved God and I loved fellowshipping with family and friends.

I grew up in a two-parent household. My parents were married but growing up with both parents didn't mean that everything at home was perfect. The house was filled with more quarrels and minimal affection. Although I knew my parents loved me and my brothers, their marital issues caused me anxiety.

I'm sure they had the normal struggles that weigh down relationships and often it would spill over into our home. I wanted love. I desired to feel love and although every family has its challenges and different things they must deal with, I was too young to escape the pain. Pain can lead you places, you never envisioned yourself. Hurt will drive you to the arms of other hurt people. My parents' struggles caused me to look for an exit. My mother always took us to church, so I learned to search for God and trust Him to help me through every situation.

I worked for everything I had. At 15, I got my first job and by 17, I was pregnant. With Christian roots firmly planted, yet still seeking love, I found Jesus and accepted Christ as my Lord and Saviour. I decided to give my life to Christ; getting baptized before my son was born. The legal age of adulthood in America is 18. I became a mother and adult simultaneously. Life as I knew it changed. Looking back, God allowed me to push through so that I can share my story and help someone else. Mark 5:27, speaks of the woman with the issue of blood pushing her way through the crowd to get to Jesus.

Being a teen mom was not easy. I had many ups and downs. I remember staying at home with my parents when I first had him, but I was determined to get my own place. I knew I could make it on my own, but I felt like it would be hard for me being a new, young mother. I did not think I could pay all the bills on my own with a baby, so I asked my friend if we could be roommates.

Now when I think about that, it is a little funny. I was not trusting God. I had some trust but was not fully trusting in Him. I got a 2-bedroom apartment and asked her to stay with me. She had her own room, and I shared a room with my son. That lasted for a few months, and she

barely stayed there. I did not feel right accepting money from her, so I found another roommate. This time it was a friend that needed a place to stay. She came with her daughter and the father of her child. Now, in my two bedrooms, were me and my son, along with my friend and her family.

Once again this lasted a short period of time, leaving me and my son alone. And that is not the end. Next, I allowed my son's father to move in. I was hoping that the whole family thing would work out. I think most of us, if not all women, want our families to be together. What I learned is if we do not do things God's way, it will not work. It may seem to work for a while, but eventually it will all come to an end. God says, "But seek ye first the kingdom of God, and his righteousness and all these things shall be added unto you." (Matthew 6:33 KJV). Once you seek God, He will add wisdom, joy, and peace to your life. God is intentional and He does things in order. We tend to complicate things because we don't like to follow rules. These rules: however, were put in place to help us and not hurt us. God wants your family together and desires for you to get married before becoming intimate and bearing children. When we choose not to follow His will, we are out of order.

I learned my lesson for a little while, until I met my daughters' father at the age of twenty-four. I allowed him to move in with me. A few months later, we broke up. I got pregnant with my daughter after the breakup. Imagine that. We didn't get back together, but I chose to keep my baby. I know people that try to make their relationship work because of the pregnancy but having a child with someone doesn't mean you are meant to be together. Those are just the choices you made. Being a single mom of two had many challenges. As if it weren't bad enough being a teen mom. Sometimes we learn lessons the hard way and often repeat the process or make the same mistakes.

There were many times I had to work multiple jobs to make ends meet. At one point I had three jobs and they were all part-time. What I can say is through it all God was there by my side. Not one time were my lights or water turned off. My rent was paid. I do remember going without cable and Wi-Fi at some point, but God kept me. My dad was also always there to help me financially when I needed him.

My children and I attended church regularly. Your foundation is important. You need a solid foundation that starts with God. He kept me and my children. I remember one hot day and I had a window air conditioner unit that would not come on. I needed the air conditioner to work. I decided to lay my hands on it and say a prayer. After I did that, the air conditioner came on. We have power and authority in Christ. You have the power to lay hands on anything and pray. You can lay hands on yourself. Expect your healing. You can speak things into existence. I know from experience that our words shape our future. I had someone to tell me when I was younger to watch what I say and not speak negative words because they become your reality. Speak those things that are not as though they already are (Romans 4:17). The words you speak can change your life whether that be good or bad. Life and death are in the power of your tongue.

There are many things I look back on and think if I had known then what I know now, I would have been so further along. However, I do know everything is about timing so maybe some things in my earlier years I was not prepared for. *Remember God still has a plan for our lives. (Jeremiah 29:11).*

I did not listen to the wisdom of the Elders, I wanted to do things my way. They tried to share wisdom with me, and I disregarded it. I thought I had things under control. I had to learn for myself. Life is a teaching lesson. Either you will listen to others, or you will learn on your own. I encourage young people to listen because the older person has already gone through the experience. On the other hand, experience can sometimes be the best teacher.

I always had a yearning deep within for the Lord. There was a pulling on me. I didn't know exactly what it was, but I just knew deep within that I needed the Lord in my life and I would often wonder why I felt this way. My grandmother shared with me that as a child, my mom always kept a Bible with her.

She said she would make space in her closet and go there to read her Bible. She searched for God at a young age, just as I did, and my daughter does as well. At four years old, my daughter memorized The Lord's Prayer. A lot of families have generational curses that are passed down, but I am happy to say this was a generational blessing that was passed down from my mother.

Being a young, single mother and raising children was hard, but God always saw me through. He blessed me with two wonderful, smart, hard-working kids. My son excelled in education. He was the first of 4 generations to not have children out of wedlock.

This was the start of a new generational blessing. At 19, he married his high school sweetheart. He was determined to do right by God and did not want to cohabitate or build a family without marriage. They have been married for six years now and I have my first grandbaby, a baby girl named Dream. She is almost four years old and such a blessing to us all. *A Dream really does come true.*

My daughter is also well educated and very intelligent. She is tenacious and vibrant and whatever she put her mind to, she was determined to do. She won several school awards. She was Miss Junior, Miss Jonesboro, and the queen of JROTC. Recently, she won a pageant and was awarded

SGA President at her HBCU. I am a proud mother. Both of my children broke the cycle of teen pregnancy! Thank you, Lord! To God be the Glory! As you can see, life has clearly presented some challenges and awards, as I go deeper into my story, I will also share some of the scriptures that helped me make it through.

Chapter 2

The Trials of Life

"I never thought I would hear the words "diabetes."

Unexpected Diagnosis

At 39, just before Mother's Day and my birthday, the doctor diagnosed me with being a pre-diabetic. My A-1C was 6.9, normal levels are between 4.7 and 6.3. Unbeknownst to me, the prognosis was inaccurate, and I had diabetes. I immediately began researching my family history and educating myself. At that time, I knew nothing about diabetes except that my dad's mom had it before she passed away and my maternal great grandmother had it also. My paternal grandmother had her leg amputated due to diabetes and my great grandmother injected insulin shots in her stomach. The only thing I recall is being extremely fatigued, with low energy. Prior to this, I thought I was pretty healthy, and only went to preventive care visits and annual exams.

Side Effects. I never thought I would hear the words "diabetes." So, imagine my surprise, when I went from being healthy to quarterly checkups, monitoring my sugar levels and being placed on Metformin. I began experiencing stomach issues caused by the medication. I lost twenty pounds taking Metformin. I was told it would go away after a few months. I stayed on the metformin for nine months, and my condition never improved. My doctor placed me on a new medication called glipizide. Once again, I had a reaction to the medication. My blood sugar levels dropped. I tried several different methods to get my levels right with the glipizide. I tried it with and without food, but I was unable to stabilize my blood sugar. At one point, I began to shake and feel dizzy. In order to elevate my levels, I had to eat or drink something.

As if things couldn't get any worse, my daughter's best friend lost his fourteen-year-old sister to cancer. After praying for her and having my pastor and others pray, she still passed away. It left me feeling lost and heartbroken for the family. I didn't understand why God allowed her to suffer so much and why she wasn't healed. I know she is with the Lord and no longer in pain, but this was not the response we were looking for. I took the passing hard.

Anxiety. Between the fear of death and coping with diabetes and a previous car accident; the anxiety was worsening. I began having heart palpitations; I was disoriented. Two months after her death, anxiety took root. I was still seeking understanding from God, but with all that had been happening in my life, fear set in. I was afraid of death, I felt as if my prayers were unanswered, I was battling multiple illnesses and I began having panic attacks.

One day I was driving a route and had no access to anything to eat or drink, so I began to panic and feel dizzy. I wasn't sure what was going on with me, whether it was my sugar level or my nerves. I was not able to check my levels while driving, so I pulled over, got a drink and a bite to eat and felt better. I had another episode with the same symptoms, it was then that I realized I could not go long without eating something.

Since I experienced too many complications from the medications and decided to try an alternative method of controlling it. I discontinued the medicine and managed my blood sugar with diet and exercise. Today, I eat on a strict schedule; having a few small meals throughout the day. My A-1C never went past 6.9. I got it down to 5.8, and I am still trying to acquire a healthier glucose range. To date, I am maintaining normal sugar levels and working even harder to keep the additional weight off.

I felt like I was falling apart. I had to pull myself together and I decided that it was time to get help and get over this fear. My daughter and I both began to go to therapy to learn how to cope with the grief we experienced.

It seemed as if as soon as I said Yes to my calling, all hell began to break loose. I had to fight through this. No matter how I felt, God said to do it anyway. It didn't matter if I was in pain, scared, confused, or didn't understand, I had to keep pushing. I remember leaving work one day because my chest was hurting, and I could barely breathe. I went to the emergency room, where they completed blood work and an elektrokardiogram – (EKG), of which the results were all normal. I was sent home and told to stop worrying. The final diagnosis was anxiety.

My anxiety got so severe that I was forced to resign from my job. Sitting at home and unable to work, took a toll on me. I dealt with it the best way I knew how. I kept praying and declaring my healing. I reached out to others to pray for me as well. While I was at home, I joined a health and wellness business. Not long after that, I heard the voice of the Lord tell me to enroll in school. I always wanted to go back to school but wasn't sure of what to major in, and I did not want to accumulate loans. God told me not to worry about the money and to trust him and not to back out.

It had been a while since I had been in school, over twenty years to be exact. I started classes at the beginning of April 2019 and received my degree in 2021! All the while, still dealing with anxiety, but nevertheless, I was determined to finish. There's opportunity in adversity. "Greater is He that is in me than he that is in the world." No weapon formed against me shall prosper." I meditated on these two scriptures daily.

Here we go again

I went in for a routine checkup and my doctor discovered something else. There was an issue found with my thyroid and I had to get a biopsy. Prior to this appointment, I was nervous. My doctor was checking out everything and having several tests done. It was not an easy task having test after test, going to all these different appointments, then waiting on the results. I began to pray for healing from any sickness or disease. God sent prayer warriors to encourage me and get me prepared for the biopsy. I even had a woman of faith check me in upon my arrival to my appointment. She was a breath of fresh air. She encouraged me, shared positive information, and reassured me. I went to the back, and after a few minutes, my name was called. I was escorted to the examination room, where I anxiously awaited the doctors' arrival. When he arrived, he explained the procedure, and had me sign paperwork. The first step was getting a shot to numb the area. Then he started the procedure. I noticed that I could not feel anything. After a few minutes, it was over. I felt a sigh of relief. All the worries and nervousness were for nothing. It was way less frightening than I expected.

These scare tactics come from Satan. He wants us to be nervous and worry instead of trusting God. Faith over fear, God was with me the whole time. Do not let Satan play mind games with you. Cover yourself with the blood of Jesus every day. Put on the whole armor of God. This is what I did daily. A lot of times we want to turn to others to pray for us, but God has given us the power and authority to pray for ourselves. Say, "I am healthy, I am whole, I am healed!" Speak "I AM" words of affirmation daily. I am a child of God, I am saved, I am beautiful, I am fearfully and wonderfully made, I can do all things through Christ.

Chapter 3
Ask, Seek, Knock

"There were many times in my life when I would ask God to help me, but I would stop there. I had an issue with trusting God. I did not want to wait on Him."

What does it mean to Ask, Seek, and Knock? God wants to give you the desires of your heart. God says Ask, and it will be given to you; seek, and you will find; knock, and the door will be opened for you. (Matthew 7:7)

Ask. There are so many times in our lives when God is just waiting on us to ask Him for help. We go through life trying to work things out in our strength when we really need the strength of God. There were many times in my life when I would ask God to help me, but I would stop there.

I had an issue with trusting God. I did not want to wait on Him. I would give God some time to work out my issues (most of the time they were issues I created) and if He did not work it out in my timing, I would pick up the problem and try to figure it out on my own. We must have patience with God. His time is not our time. God can turn things around in a minute, an hour, or a day. We cannot give our problems to God and then take them back. Whenever I did that, it did not work in my favor. I could have been much further along if I had trusted God and believed in His promises, rather than trying to be God and solve the problem. I would not have to ask God for anything if I could do it myself. Little did I know, I was prolonging my future by trying to handle my issues on my own. Getting two steps ahead, then going back four. God is faithful. He will not fail you. You can put your trust in Him, He is not like man. Trusting Him will take time, faith, and surrender. When you ask and believe, God will answer your prayers, but they never come to you the way you think they should.

Seek. 1 Chronicles 16:11 says, Seek the Lord and His strength; Seek His face continually. God is there if we seek

ASK, SEEK, KNOCK

Him. To seek God, is to pray to Him, read His word, talk to Him first, before you make any moves or decisions.

Have you ever looked at your life and wondered, "why is it taking me so long to get somewhere?" Are you trying to do things on your own or are you seeking God for answers; allowing Him to lead, guide, and direct you? God will allow us to make our own decisions. He is a God of choices. His Word instructs us to choose life or death and which master we will serve.

Knock. When you knock on God's door, you are requesting something from Him. It's in expectation that He will open the door and meet your needs. In order for God to open the door, you must be determined to get what you are petitioning Him for. In the book of Genesis, Jacob told the angel, I will not let you go unless you bless me. Once we ask God to help us and show us the way, we must then act on it. When you ask for something, God may give you dreams, visions or steps to guide you. I like to keep a journal and write down my prayer requests, instructions, and Bible verses similar to what I desire. His Word says don't grow weary in your well doing, though it tarries wait for it. There are seasons when you will have to be still and wait on God. Those times can become very difficult. This may cause you to grow impatient and get tired. During those times you can still do something. Pray and have a timeline. Write in a calendar to keep up with what you want to do. If you need help, do not be afraid to ask for help. Asking is being dependent on God. Seeking is an indication that you desire Him. Knocking is being diligent. Do not stop until you get what you prayed for, but remember God knows best, so it may not look exactly the way you pictured it.

Reasons Why Sometimes We Do Not Ask, Seek, Or Knock

We procrastinate for different reasons. You might be tired, overwhelmed, fearful or even unmotivated. Results of this may show up through lack of sleep, visual clutter, mental clutter, unbalanced priorities, depression, outside noise, other people, lack of exercise, or dehydration. For twenty-one days try to create a habit that becomes a lifestyle. Some habits can include prayer, exercise, reading the Bible, drinking water, eating fruit/vegetables daily, open mail every day, and spend at least fifteen minutes of quality time with family/kids. Begin to ask yourself how bad do you want it and how strong is your faith? Be persistent.

Chapter 4

Spiritual Gifts

"God does not make mistakes in our lives, no matter how long it takes to do His will."

According to a test I took while in school, my top three spiritual gifts are evangelism, prophecy, and apostleship. These are gifts of the fivefold ministry. Ephesians 4:11-13, says...So, Christ himself gave the apostles, the prophets, the evangelists, the pastors and teachers, to equip his people for works of service, so that the body of Christ may be built up until we all reach unity in the faith and in the knowledge of the Son of God and become mature, attaining to the whole measure of the fullness of Christ.

Evangelism. Evangelism is spreading the good news about Christ to the world. It is helping the lost souls understand why He (Jesus) came from heaven to earth. It is about winning souls for the Kingdom of God. There are many ways to evangelize and share with others. Some examples are: preaching, church crusades, counseling, and Bible study. This office is not something you go to school for; however, God gives the church an Evangelist as a gift. Evangelists teach salvation for all mankind through God's one and only son, Jesus Christ. Matthew, Mark, Luke, and John are believed to have been Evangelists, but there is mention of one in the Bible, Philip, that is called an evangelist. Acts 21:8, says, And the next *day* we that were of Paul's company departed, and came unto Cæsarea: and we entered into the house of Philip the evangelist, which was *one* of the seven; and abode with him.

Evangelism is demonstrated in many ways. I exercise my gift by talking with family and friends about things they may not know pertaining to the body of Christ.

In some instances, I plant seeds into their lives and provide a better understanding about salvation and God's

Word. Once the seed is planted, God will water it. That means He will make sure His children get what they need to mature in Him. I have also invited several people to church over time and have witnessed them get saved, baptized, or rededicate their lives to God.

Prophecy. A prophet, also known as a seer, is appointed by God. I've had dreams and there are times when God speaks to me regarding people. Sometimes the Holy Spirit will lead me to share what God said to me regarding an individual. There are different types of prophets and prophetic gifts demonstrated throughout the Bible: Nahum, Habakkuk, Zephania, to name a few. Prophecy is supernatural, divine, and purposeful, coming directly from the throne of God. At this current time I have not been called to the office of a prophet. I am seeking God and studying this gift.

Apostleship. An Apostle is referred to as a sent one. This position is not appointed by man, rather it is established by the Holy Spirit and is the highest office in ministry. One that possesses this gift must have all five of the gifts of the fivefold ministry: Apostle, Prophet, Evangelist, Pastor, and Teacher. One of the most popular Apostles in the Bible was Paul, though there were many before him. Apostleship is planting churches or ministries; I am humbly asking God where and when to start the ministries. I like to assist and help others. Whether the help is physical, mental, or spiritual. God will lead and I will follow His will. I have taken the spiritual gifts test previously and the result of evangelism is the same. I took one when I was twenty-two years old, and my gifts were encouragement, hospitality, and evangelism. I also had one in my thirties, and now in my forties. Prophecy and apostleship are new results. I believe the reason for that is because I have spiritually grown in Christ. When I said yes to the Lord, I meant it. The road has been difficult, but I will not give up. I will allow God to use me according to His Will.

My test results of the apostleship surprised me because I did not have a clear understanding of the word. After reading about it in its entirety, I understand why it registered as one of my gifts. I do believe the test for me is right on. It showed me how all my spiritual gifts work together to accomplish God's will. This is a gift that I am currently not operating in but hope to in the near future. God does not make mistakes in our lives, no matter how long it takes to do His will. I would love to start ministries to be able to assist and help others.

I have always had an interest in sharing the Good News about Christ. I have always had a desire to tell my family and friends about being saved, not wanting anyone left behind.

I will be the best steward of Christ that I can be by obeying whatever God asks of me. If it is speaking, I will speak. If it is to hear His voice and prophesy, I will do it. God will lead and I will follow His will. He continues to build us for His glory. Jesus was our example of servanthood. He came to serve others. Everything we know about God and ministry, we learned from Jesus (Yeshua). He was the greatest and the only perfect example on earth.

You may still be asking "how do I glow from it?" Just be the best you can be no matter what circumstances you face, what trials you go through, or what obstacles come your way. You can still come out of it glowing. Write the books, start the business, buy the home. Continue to Grow and Glow.

Chapter 5

Disciplining Yourself

"I realized out of those 1440 minutes in a day, I spent most of that time worrying, and not in God's Word or trusting Him."

No discipline seems pleasant at the time, but painful. Later on, however, it produces a harvest of righteousness and peace for those who have been trained by it (Hebrew 12:11). We will not be able to go higher if we do not let go and let God take control and lead the way. My number one fear in my twenties was having thoughts of my past, present, and future altogether instead of dealing with things one day at a time. It was a struggle, but I remember telling myself that God knows what is best for me. He would not bring me this far to leave me. Just trust Him and let Him be the captain of your ship. When God was teaching the Israelites to let go of their idols, He took them through the wilderness. A lot of times we try to make old things like new ones when God is saying destroy them! Sometimes we are our own biggest enemy, we must let go and let God. God will not leave us, but He will correct us. Every day we gain new mercy because of God's compassion and love for us. We may experience some pain during our discipline, but it will make us stronger believers in the end. We must remember what God has done for us, and thank Him every morning.

Key elements to walking in Discipline- 3 T's
(Time, Trust, and Thankfulness)

Time management. Investing most of my time in God is what I am doing these days. Even when I am doing other things like resting, watching tv, grocery shopping, or anything else God is still at the forefront of my mind. Now, this is not something that happened overnight, it is a learned behavior that developed over time. After messing up so many times and wondering why I could not get things right, I had to examine myself and take note of how I was spending my time.

I realized out of those 1440 minutes in a day, I spent most of that time worrying, and not in God's Word or trusting Him. I was just wasting time. I wanted to see a change in my life, so I had to make changes. God wants us to invest time in Him. There is room for improvement, so keep pressing and pushing to get to where you need to be in Christ. It is an everyday process. After much prayer, I realized God wants to be involved in every choice or decision we make.

Now my days are filled with more reading, praying, worshiping, exercising (focusing on health), devotionals, online studying, and fellowshipping with other believers. I have also allotted more time for my children and my granddaughter. Family is your first ministry, and it is very important to make time for them also.

Being in school and studying was another way I chose to invest my time. It helped me learn how to build the Kingdom and accomplish God's mission here on earth. What we do for Christ helps the Kingdom. Only what we do for Him matters in the end. When we stand before Christ, He will not ask us how many pairs of shoes we have, or how many cars we own; He will ask how many people did you save, how many seeds did you sow into others, did you feed the hungry, and did you serve others? All these things help build the Kingdom of God. Being a good steward of time is one of the most important investments as a child of God.

Trust God (Yahweh). Trusting God takes discipline. Since we are born in sin, and God gives us free will, it may take time to learn to trust Him. It takes supernatural strength to trust God. Fully trusting God is a process. Throughout my life I have experienced hurt. Hurt is one way that the devil keeps us from trusting in God. Satan knows if people hurt us, disown, or use us, we somehow think God will treat us the same way. But God is not like man. He is our Savior, our provider, our peace, our healer, our all in all, my everything. Except God's love today.

God was there when I needed Him. Even when I did not feel Him around me. God has healed me, delivered me, and set me free from other people and myself. Keep trusting God. In the past few years, this pandemic has shown me another face of God and I had to learn how to trust Him in a new way. I remember watching the news and seeing so many perish that it moved me to tears. I learned to trust God no matter what. I learned to pray about everything, no matter how big or small it may seem. Call out to God, He will hear you. I am learning not to take on too much at once. I had to stay focused on my purpose. I could not let what was going on distract me. My prayer was, Lord let me live in purpose and on purpose every day. I had to learn that things will come and go, but God will remain forever. I try to catch distractions as soon as they come and immediately come against them in prayer. Praying for yourself and others is important. It is how you protect yourself against the attacks of the enemy.

Thankfulness. In every situation, give thanks. Train yourself to be thankful no matter what. Paul puts it this way in Philippians **4:11,** Not that I speak in respect of want: for I have learned, in whatsoever state I am, *therewith* to be content.

A grateful heart goes a long way. Most of us grew up being taught to say please and thank you. We should be thankful for one another and mostly God. I have had to discipline my mind to be thankful when things were not going the way I wanted it to go. There are so many things to be thankful for. I am thankful I made it through; thankful to be strong and healthy; thankful that I am in my right mind, thankful my children are well. Wake up and say thank you Lord. Thank you for another day. What are you thankful for?

Allow God to Flow Through You

One area I need to work on is allowing God to flow through me. Sometimes I second-guess myself, unsure of what to say, when I feel I'm being led by God. We must learn to let the Holy Spirit guide and lead us. We do not have to push our God on others but allow God to give us a listening ear, discernment, and the right words to say. It is important to be emotionally stable when helping others. You cannot help others if you are just as distraught or emotional as they are. Allow God to strengthen you and build you up. Remember and recite this verse daily, I can do all things through Christ who gives me strength (Philippians 4:13). I will live with boldness, power, and in the anointing of the Holy Spirit. God has called all of us to serve. We can do this service graciously with His help. **Grow through it and Glow from it!**

Renew your mind daily with these Scriptures that helped me Grow & Glow

Fear not, for I am with you; Be not dismayed, for I am your God. I will strengthen you, yes, I will help you, I will uphold you with My righteous right hand. (Isaiah 41:10).

"And be not conformed to this world: but be ye transformed by the renewing of your mind, that ye may prove what is that good, and acceptable, and perfect, will of God." (Romans 12:2 KJV).

There is therefore now no condemnation to those who are in Christ Jesus, who do not walk according to the flesh, but according to the Spirit. (Romans 8:1).

For I know the thoughts that I think toward you, says the Lord, thoughts of peace and not of evil, to give you a future and a hope. (Jeremiah 29:11-13).

Or what man is there among you who, if his son asks for bread, will give him a stone? Or if he asks for a fish, will he give him a serpent? If you then, being evil, know how to give good gifts to your children, how much more will your

Father who is in heaven give good things to those who ask Him. (Matthew 7:9-11).

For I am persuaded that neither death nor life, nor angels nor principalities nor powers, nor things present nor things to come, nor height nor depth, nor any other created thing, shall be able to separate us from the love of God which is in Christ Jesus our Lord. (Romans 8:38-39).

But those who wait on the Lord shall renew their strength; they shall mount up with wings like eagles, they shall run and not be weary. They shall walk and not faint. (Isaiah 40:31).

For He, Himself has said, "I will never leave nor forsake you. (Hebrews 13:5).

For God has not given us a spirit of fear, but of power and love and a sound mind. (2 Timothy 1:7).

But without faith, it is impossible to please Him, for he who comes to God must believe that He is and that He is a rewarder of those who diligently seek Him. (Hebrews 11:6).

He gives power to the weak, and to those who have no might, He increases strength. (Isaiah 40:29).

He who dwells in the secret place of the highest shall abide under the shadow of the Almighty. I will say of the Lord, "He is my refuge and my fortress; My God, in Him I will trust." (Psalm 91:1&2).

Have I not commanded you? Be strong and of good courage; do not be afraid, nor be dismayed, for the Lord your God is with you wherever you go. (Joshua 1:9).

Ask, and it will be given to you; seek, and you will find; knock, and it will be opened to you. For everyone who asks receives, and he who seeks finds, and to him who knocks, it will be opened. (Matthew 7:7&8).

Yea though I walk through the valley of the shadow of death, I will fear no evil; For You are with me; Your rod and Your staff, they comfort me. (Psalm 23:4).

Being confident of this very thing, that He who has begun a good work in you will complete it until the day of Jesus Christ. (Philippians 1:6).

I know how to be abased, and I know how to abound. Everywhere and in all things, I have learned both to be full and to be hungry, both to abound and to suffer need. I can do all things through Christ who strengthens me. (Philippians 4:12&13).

The Lord is my light and my salvation; Whom shall, I fear? The Lord is the strength of my life; Of whom shall I be afraid. (Psalm 27:1).

These scriptures will help you to overcome if you just trust God. God must be our source, the one whom we trust and believe.

"Trust in the Lord with all your heart and lean not on your understanding; In all your ways acknowledge Him, And He shall direct your paths." (Proverbs 3:5-6)

"Be anxious for nothing, but in everything by prayer and supplication, with thanksgiving let your requests be made known to God. And the peace of God, which surpasses all understanding, will guard your hearts and minds through Christ Jesus." (Philippians 4:6-7)

Prayer of Salvation

"If you would like to be saved or rededicate your life to Christ, say this prayer with me.
"Lord please forgive me for my sins, you know all about me. I repent and want to live right. I believe Jesus died for me and rose on the 3rd day. I accept Jesus as my Lord and Savior."

If you said this prayer and believe this in your heart, You Are Saved! It is just that simple. Now begin to read the word of God and get connected to people who are teaching the truth about Christ. Contact me with any questions or let me know about your new walk. (2 Corinthians 5:17 ESV) says, Therefore, if anyone is in Christ, he is a new creation. The old has passed away; behold, the new has come. You may also want to get baptized by water and by the filling of the Holy Spirit. To God be the Glory. Blessings to you and your family and welcome to the Kingdom of God! Thank you, Lord. (**Adonai**)

About the Author

Takesha Brown is a native of Louisville, Kentucky; now residing in Georgia. She is a mother of 2 adult children and a grandmother to her pride and joy, Dream. A recent college graduate in the school of Divinity, Takesha holds a ministerial degree obtained while she was going through some of life's most challenging times. After hearing the voice of God speak to her about putting inspirational quotes on shirts, she launched a business customizing T-shirts and accessories and began selling her apparel on her website **tbquotes.com**. You can also get inspiration by following her on Instagram **@tbquotesinspiration** or **Facebook-Inspirational Quotes and on Clubhouse: Takesha Brown**. In April of 2020, a few months after the pandemic started, she ventured into writing and is destined to become a household name with her introductory book, Grow through it and Glow from it.

Acknowledgments

I dedicate this book to you Lord, for without you none of this would be possible. Thank you for your grace and mercy and for the many gifts you have bestowed upon me. To my parents, I thank God for using you to give me life and for instilling in me the principles and foundation of God. If not for you two, I would not be here today. A very special thank you to my son Kahlill, his wife Marie, my granddaughter Dream, and my daughter Destiney. I love and adore each and everyone of you. You give me so many reasons to keep praying, fighting, and persevering. Lord knows where I would be, if it had not been for the Lord on my side. I thank you for your love and support. Apostle Shirley, whom I recently met, thank you for your words of life and encouragement, which birthed the title of this book.

She told me once I grow, I will glow. I had another title before speaking with her, but after she said "Glow from it" I immediately wrote the words down and told her I would use that as a part of my book title. Dr. Kishma, words cannot express how grateful I am for your push. Lastly, to all my family and friends who have been there for me throughout this entire process, I sincerely thank you from the bottom of my heart.

Connect with Author Takesha Brown

Takeshabrown1@gmail.com

Keshb07@yahoo.com

Website - tbquotes.com

Instagram - @tbquotesinspiration

Facebook - Inspirational Quotes

Clubhouse - Takesha Brown

All Books available on Amazon.com

NOTES

NOTES

Made in the USA
Columbia, SC
15 February 2023